Sisters in Crime
Los Angeles Chapter

Desserticide

aka
Desserts Worth Dying For

Edited by
Claire Carmichael, Paulette Mouchet, and Mary Terrill

Crown Valley Press
P.O. Box 336
Acton, CA 93510-0336
(805) 269-1525

Legal Notice and Disclaimer

Although every effort has been made to ensure correctness, the recipes in this book may contain errors and omissions. Specific poison dosage information has deliberately been omitted. All material contained in this book is for entertainment purposes only.

The editors, contributors, publisher, and distributors accept no liability for any errors or omissions in this book or for any injuries or losses incurred or resulting from use of the information and recipes in this book.

Interior layout and design by Crown Valley Press.
Cover design by Gayle Partlow, Altadena, CA.

First Edition, Fourth Printing (with new cover and interior design), 1996.

ISBN 0-9647945-2-7

Preface

Thank you for purchasing our cookbook. In addition to the great recipes, we hope you enjoy our tongue-in-cheek advice for the would-be murderer.

The Los Angeles Chapter of Sisters in Crime is dedicated to promoting published and pre-published writers. With your support, we can offer new programs to meet this goal and continue to fund projects such as our anthology and No Crime Unpublished Writers' Conference.

We want to thank the members, spouses, and friends who submitted recipes and otherwise supported this project. Without their enthusiasm, this cookbook would have been nothing more than a great idea. Special thanks to Sheila Jefferson, George Mouchet, and Gayle Partlow for the stunning new cover design.

Claire Carmichael
Paulette Mouchet
Mary Terrill

Contributors

The following Sisters, Brothers, and friends contributed recipes; page numbers for their recipes follow the names.

Sybil Baker, 109
Kathleen Beaver, 105
Betty Bunn, 65
Faye Cadmus, 57
Susan B. Casmier, 83
Michele Curley, 85
Nancy Farris, 75
Jennifer Fuller, 15, 17, 21, 23, 25, 29
Charlene Gallagher, 55
Kevin Gillogly, 95
Jeanne Hartman, 81
Larry Hill, 117
Mary T. Johnson, 43, 47, 49
Rosa Felsenburg Kaplan, 63
Cynthia Lawrence, 71
Paulette Mouchet, 11, 13, 27, 45

Joe Neri, 39
Kris Neri, 31, 99
Gayle Partlow, 87
Barbara Pronin, 67, 91
Lisa Seidman, 79, 93, 103
Sandy Siegel, 33
Judith K. Smith, 35, 37, 59, 61
Susan M. Stephenson, 51, 53, 69
Mary Terrill, 19, 113
Jamie Wallace, 89, 97
Mae Woods, 41, 77, 101, 107, 111
Anita Zelman, 73

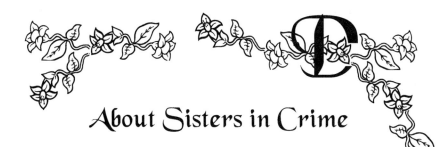

About Sisters in Crime

Sisters in Crime began in 1986 at the Baltimore Bouchercon when a number of women who read, write, buy, or sell mysteries met for an impromptu breakfast to discuss their mutual concerns. At a minimum, they hoped to develop camaraderie and to learn what women in the mystery field really wanted. There was a perception that women writers were reviewed less frequently and that their books were taken less seriously than those written by men.

Sara Paretsky was the driving force in galvanizing and organizing the group. In May of 1987, the first steering committee was elected.

In 1989, in keeping with the desire to be *for* its members, Sisters in Crime redoubled its efforts toward networking, publicizing its members' work, and lending mutual support.

The purpose of Sisters in Crime is to combat discrimination against women in the mystery field, educate publishers and the general public as to inequalities in the treatment of female authors, and raise the level of awareness of their contribution to the field.

Membership in Sisters in Crime is open to all persons worldwide who have a special interest in mystery writing and in furthering the purposes of Sisters in Crime.

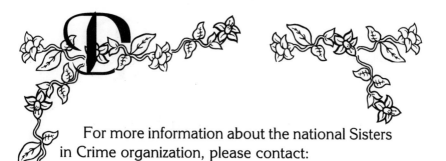

For more information about the national Sisters in Crime organization, please contact:

M. Beth Wasson, Executive Secretary
P.O. Box 442124
Lawrence, KS 66044-8933
(913) 842-1325

For more information about the Los Angeles Chapter of Sisters in Crime, please contact:

Sisters in Crime
Los Angeles Chapter
P.O. Box 251646
Los Angeles, CA 90025
(213) 694-2972

Table of Contents

An honorable murder, if you will:
For naught I did in hate, but all in honor.

Shakespeare: *Othello*, Act IV, Scene 3

Swift Dispatch Cake

2 cups	flour
1-3/4 cups	sugar
2 teaspoons	baking soda
1 teaspoon	salt
2 teaspoons	cinnamon
1 cup	coconut
1 cup	chopped nuts
2 cups	shredded carrots
1 large can	crushed pineapple in own juice
1 cup	oil
3 large	eggs
1 teaspoon	vanilla

Preheat oven to 350 degrees Fahrenheit. Grease a 9x13-inch glass *cake* pan.

With a *wooden* spoon, mix together all ingredients in a large, *glass* bowl. Pour into cake pan. Bake 1 hour or until a toothpick inserted in the center comes out clean. Frost with It's a Killer Frosting when cool.

It's a Killer Frosting

6 ounces	cream cheese, softened
1/4 cup (1/2 stick)	butter, softened
2 cups	powdered sugar
1 teaspoon	vanilla

Cream together the cream cheese and butter. Add powdered sugar and vanilla. Beat until smooth.

Some poison'd by their wives...

Shakespeare: *Richard II,* Act III

In the extreme instances of reaction against convention,
female murderers get sheaves of offers of marriage.

George Bernard Shaw: Preface to *Getting Married*

Coup de Grace
Cranberry Salad

1 cup	water and reserved pineapple juice
1 large box	raspberry gelatin
1 1-pound can	whole cranberry sauce
8 ounces	ginger ale
1 13-1/2-ounce can	crushed pineapple, drain and reserve juice

In a 2-quart saucepan bring water and pineapple juice to a boil. Add raspberry gelatin and stir to dissolve. Add cranberry sauce, ginger ale, and crushed pineapple. Pour into 9x9x2-inch pan and chill until firm. Spread topping over salad.

Topping

1 8-ounce package	Dream Whip
8 ounces	cream cheese, softened

Whip Dream Whip and cream cheese together until smooth.

Murder, though it have no tongue,
Will speak with most miraculous organ.

Shakespeare: *Hamlet,* Act II, Scene 2

Other sins only speak; murder shrieks out.

John Webster: *Duchess of Malfi,* Act IV

Poisoned Apple Cake

Stepmother's special.

3 cups	flour
1 teaspoon	salt
1-1/2 teaspoons	baking soda
1-1/4 cups	oil
2 cups	sugar
2 large	eggs
3 teaspoons	vanilla
1 cup	chopped nuts
3 cups	finely chopped apples
	sugar
	cinnamon

Preheat oven to 350 degrees Fahrenheit. Grease a 9x13-inch cake pan.

Sift together the flour, salt, and soda. Set aside. Mix the oil, sugar, eggs, and vanilla together until smooth. Add the flour mixture and mix until blended. Add the nuts and apples. Stir until blended. Pour into cake pan. Sprinkle the top with sugar and cinnamon. Bake 1 hour or until a toothpick inserted in the center comes out clean.

Arsenic:
The King of Poisons

A metallic poison naturally occurring in lead and iron ore, used widely since ancient times, and known as "the king of poisons." Arsenic is a white, tasteless powder that resembles powdered sugar or flour. Arsenic has one other helpful quality—it is cumulative, so many small doses can be given over time. Be aware, however, that tolerance builds up (see Dorothy Sayers' *Strong Poison*, which utilized this fact in the plot).

Another reason that poisoners have been so keen to use arsenic is that the symptoms mimic ordinary illnesses, such as food poisoning.

Poisoners using arsenic are advised to encourage cremation of their victims, as arsenic remains in the body, which can lead to an accurate estimation of when administration of the poison began.

Hack and Chop Layer Cake

Now I layer me down to die...

1 cup	flour
1/2 cup (1 stick)	butter (not margarine)
1/2 cup	chopped nuts
1 cup	Cool Whip
1 cup	powdered sugar
8 ounces	cream cheese
2 small boxes	instant lemon or chocolate pudding mix
3 cups	milk
1 large tub	Cool Whip
	chopped nuts or maraschino cherries

Preheat oven to 350 degrees Fahrenheit. Grease a 9x13-inch cake pan.

Cut the butter into the flour. Stir in the nuts. Press into the cake pan. Bake 15 minutes. Cool. Mix 1 cup Cool Whip, powdered sugar, and cream cheese together and spread over baked layer. Beat instant pudding and milk together until thick. Spread over Cool Whip layer. Top with 1 large tub of Cool Whip. Garnish with nuts or maraschino cherries.

Feigning Amnesia to Avoid a Murder Rap

There are two kinds of amnesia: retrograde and anterograde. Retrograde amnesia occurs after a blow to the head or the experience of some shocking event. Memory is lost for the events immediately preceding the injury. Anterograde amnesia occurs when the victim loses all memories after an event and is unable to efficiently form new memories, but otherwise functions naturally.

Murderers are advised to be afflicted by retrograde amnesia in order to utilize the "everything went black and now I can't remember a thing" defense.

Don't Leave Your Jam Thumbprints! Cookies

1 cup (2 sticks)	butter or margarine
2/3 cup	sugar
1 teaspoon	vanilla
1/2 teaspoon	lemon extract
2 large	eggs
2-1/2 cups	flour
1/2 teaspoon	salt
	thick jam, any flavor

Preheat oven to 375 degrees Fahrenheit. Grease cookie sheets.

Cream butter and sugar. Blend in vanilla, lemon extract, eggs, flour, and salt. Beat well. Form into 1-inch balls. Place on cookie sheets. Make depression in center of each ball and fill with jam. Pinch together. Bake 13 minutes. Remove from cookie sheet and cool on racks.

Disposing of the Body: Secret Burial

Although this may appear an acceptable option, secret burial presents some serious difficulties.

First, it may be difficult to locate suitable ground, particularly in urban areas, and transporting a body for long distances in a vehicle can cause you trouble with law enforcement agencies.

Second, digging a grave of adequate depth is very hard work and will require appropriate tools—at the very least a pick and large shovel. Also, even if you are digging a six-foot hole in your own backyard, neighbors can often exhibit the most inconvenient curiosity as to what you are doing.

Third, after the body is buried, there will always be evidence that the ground has been disturbed in a body-sized area. Also take into account that a substantial quantity of soil will be left over.

Ax-Murderer's Banana Split Cake

Violence to bananas and pineapples!

1 cup	flour
1/4 cup	brown sugar, packed
1/3 cup	butter
1/2 cup	walnuts, chopped
2 cup	powdered sugar
1/2 cup (1 stick)	butter
2 large	eggs or equivalent egg substitute
1 large can	crushed pineapple, drained
3-4 large	bananas, sliced
1 regular size	Cool Whip
	walnuts, chopped

Preheat oven to 350 degrees Fahrenheit. Grease a 9x13-inch cake pan.

Combine flour and brown sugar. Cut in 1/3 cup butter. Stir in 1/2 cup nuts. Press into cake pan and bake 12 to 15 minutes. Cool completely. Beat powdered sugar, 1/2 cup butter, and eggs until fluffy and spread over cake. Spread crushed pineapple evenly over the top. Cover pineapple with banana slices. Top with Cool Whip. Garnish with chopped walnuts.

Interrogation Techniques: Good Guy-Bad Guy

Anyone who watches television is aware of the good guy-bad guy interrogation technique, which works well, especially with first-time offenders.

Two investigators are needed, one playing the "rogue cop," the other "considerate and understanding." They work hard to give the impression there is real conflict between them. When the rogue cop walks out of the interrogation and slams the door, the "good cop" shows sympathy and kindness, often inducing the unsuspecting murderer to confide more than intended.

Do not fall for this scenario. It is always a set-up. Both investigators are working to have you incriminate yourself.

Potent Potion Peach Cake

1 cup	flour
1 teaspoon	baking powder
1/2 teaspoon	salt
1/2 cup (1 stick)	margarine or butter
2/3 cup	sugar
2 large	eggs
1 teaspoon	vanilla
1 tablespoon	peach syrup
3 ounces	cream cheese
1/3 cup	sugar
1/4 cup	sour cream
1 large	egg
1 29-ounce can	sliced peaches, drained; reserve syrup
1 cup	sour cream
2 tablespoons	brown sugar

Preheat oven to 350 degrees Fahrenheit. Grease a 10-inch pie pan.

Combine flour, baking powder, and salt. Set aside. Cream together margarine and 2/3 cup sugar. Add 2 eggs and beat well. Stir in flour mixture, vanilla, and peach syrup until blended. Spread evenly in the bottom and sides of pie pan. Set aside. Mix together cream cheese and 1/3 cup sugar. Beat in sour cream and 1 egg. Pour into the middle of the flour mixture in the pie pan. Bake 30 to 35 minutes. Remove from oven. Arrange peach slices on top of baked cake. Mix sour cream and brown sugar. Pour over peaches and put cake back in the oven for 5 minutes. Cool and chill.

Digitalis

A useful poison that brings about death by heart failure and thus looks like the victim has suffered an unfortunate heart attack.

Digitalis is extracted from the leaves of the foxglove plant (*Digitalis purpurea*) and was used for many years in very small doses to regulate heart rhythms. In larger doses it is fatal within two or three hours.

Running Berserk Brandy Cake

Go extract crazy!

3 cups	sugar
1 cup (2 sticks)	butter
6 large	eggs
3 cups	flour
1/4 teaspoon	baking soda
1/4 teaspoon	salt
1 cup	sour cream
1/2 teaspoon	rum extract
1/2 teaspoon	almond extract
1 teaspoon	orange extract
1/2 teaspoon	lemon extract
1 teaspoon	vanilla
1/2 cup	apricot brandy or apricot nectar

Preheat oven to 325 degrees Fahrenheit. Grease and flour the bottom of a large tube pan.

Cream together butter and sugar. Add the eggs one at a time, beating after each addition. Sift together flour, soda, and salt. In a separate bowl, combine sour cream, extracts, and brandy or nectar. Add the flour and sour cream mixtures alternately to the butter-sugar mixture. Mix until blended. Pour into tube pan and bake 70 minutes or until a toothpick inserted in the center comes out clean.

To die will be an awfully big adventure.

James M. Barrie: *Peter Pan*

Layer Me in the Grave Cookies

1/2 cup (1 stick)	butter
1 cup	graham cracker crumbs
6 ounces	semisweet chocolate chips
6 ounces	butterscotch chips
1 cup	coconut, shredded
1 can	sweetened condensed milk
1 cup	walnuts, chopped

Preheat oven to 350 degrees Fahrenheit.

Melt butter in a 9x13-inch cake pan. Spread graham cracker crumbs evenly in pan. Layer the chocolate chips, butterscotch chips, and coconut, in order, over crumbs. Drizzle sweetened condensed milk over all. Top with chopped walnuts. Bake 30 minutes. Cut into bars.

The Crime Scene

The first priority of police officers at a crime scene is to preserve the area from any possible contamination and to keep all physical evidence from being altered or destroyed.

Of course, your intention as a murderer is precisely the opposite. For this reason, it is advisable to encourage as many people as possible to enter the crime scene prior to the arrival of the authorities. Neighbors, friends, and relatives can be called. A quick anonymous call to the media may be useful. Once the police arrive, demand a religious advisor and/or doctor.

Always remember that the more people who enter a crime scene, the more compromised the evidence (against you) will be!

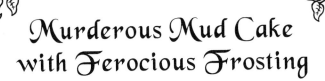

Murderous Mud Cake
with Ferocious Frosting

4 large	eggs
2 cups	sugar
1 cup (2 sticks)	butter, melted
1-1/2 cups	flour
1/3 cup	cocoa powder
1 cup	walnuts, chopped
1 7-ounce jar	marshmallow creme
3 ounces	cream cheese, softened

Preheat oven to 350 degrees Fahrenheit. Grease and flour a 9x13-inch cake pan.

Beat together the eggs and sugar. Mix in melted butter, flour, cocoa powder, and walnuts. Pour into cake pan. Bake 30 minutes until cake tests done. Blend together marshmallow cream and cream cheese. Spread over hot cake. Allow to cool. Frost with Ferocious Frosting.

Ferocious Frosting

1/3 cup	cocoa powder
1/2 cup (1 stick)	butter
6 tablespoons	milk
3 ounces	cream cheese
1 teaspoon	vanilla
1 pound	powdered sugar
	walnuts, chopped

Cream together all ingredients, except walnuts, and spread over cooled cake. Garnish with chopped walnuts.

Castor Bean

The castor bean (*Ricinus communis*), a.k.a. castor oil plant or palma-christi, is a common ornamental houseplant originally from Africa. In the garden, it may reach fifteen feet in height. It has large, deeply lobed leaves and insignificant flowers.

A few seeds will produce symptoms of severe poisoning, a few more will be fatal...

Baneful Bread and Butter Pudding with Last Gasp Sauce

8 slices	French bread
3 tablespoons	butter or margarine
1/3 cup	light brown sugar, packed
1 teaspoon	cinnamon
1/3 cup	walnuts, chopped
1/3 cup	semisweet chocolate chips
3 large	eggs, slightly beaten
1/3 cup	granulated sugar
1/2 teaspoon	vanilla
dash	salt
2-1/4 cups	milk, scalded
1/4 cup	Irish cream liqueur
	Last Gasp Sauce (recipe follows)

Heat oven to 350 degrees Fahrenheit. Butter a 1-1/2 quart casserole.

Toast bread slices slightly and spread butter on one side of each. Sprinkle with brown sugar, cinnamon, chopped nuts, and chocolate chips. Press slices of bread together, forming four sandwiches. Cut off crusts, then cut into rectangular strips. Arrange strips in casserole. Blend eggs, granulated sugar, salt, vanilla, and liqueur. Gradually stir in scalded milk. Pour mixture over bread. Place casserole in a pan of very hot water (1-inch deep) and bake 65 to 70 minutes or until a knife inserted in the center comes out clean. Serve pudding warm or cold with Last Gasp Sauce.

(Continued)

Last Gasp Sauce

6 tablespoons	butter or margarine
1/2 cup	granulated sugar
1 large	egg
	Irish cream liqueur to taste

Cream butter and sugar. Cook in a double boiler until sugar is well dissolved. Partially cool and add beaten egg. Whip quickly so egg does not curdle. Cool and add liqueur to taste. Whip before serving and pour over pudding.

Cold Killer Compote

Slice and dice to good effect!

1 large can each   pears
         peaches
         chunk pineapple
         mandarin oranges
         cherry pie filling

Preheat oven to 325 degrees Fahrenheit.

Drain the pears, peaches, pineapple, and oranges in a colander for 4 hours. Quarter the pears and peaches—an excellent opportunity to sharpen your slicing skills—then mix together with the pineapple and oranges. Place in a 2-quart, oven-proof glass bowl. Pour the cherry pie filling over the top. Do not stir in the pie filling. Bake 1 hour.

This hot variation of a cold favorite can also be served as a side dish—in case you don't want your guests hanging around for dessert

Aconitine

A vegetable alkaloid poison derived from *Aconitum napellus,* the wolfsbane or monkshood plant. The leaf looks like parsley and the root like horseradish. Its bitter taste must be disguised—a sweet confection will do the trick!

In solution, it can be absorbed through the skin and was greatly favored in ancient Greece and Rome as a means of removing inconvenient people, particularly politicians.

Sweet Revenge Chocolate Bars

This yummy confection would easily disguise
a bitter white poison
sprinkled on top along with the powdered sugar.

1 cup + 2 tablespoons	flour
1-1/2 cups	brown sugar
1/2 cup (1 stick)	butter or margarine
1/2 teaspoon	baking powder
1 teaspoon	vanilla
1/4 teaspoon	salt
1 12-ounce package	semisweet chocolate chips
2 large	eggs, beaten
	powdered sugar and ???

Preheat oven to 350 degrees Fahrenheit. Butter a 9x13-inch cake pan.

Sift together 1 cup flour and 1/2 cup brown sugar. Cut in the butter or margarine until the mixture has pie-crust consistency. Pat the mixture in the bottom of cake pan. Bake until slightly brown. While this crust is baking, combine the remaining 1 cup brown sugar and 2 tablespoons flour. Add baking powder, vanilla, salt, chocolate chips, and eggs. Mix well. Spread evenly on baked crust and continue baking for 20 minutes. Cool. Sprinkle with powdered sugar. Cut into bars.

Mushrooms and Toadstools

Look for brown mushrooms with purple-brown or pink gills below the cap. These can be quite deadly. Some have very delayed symptoms, which might be useful.

Deadly cort (*Cortinarius gentilis*) produces symptoms of kidney failure that do not appear until two to three weeks after ingestion. This fungus, usually found under conifer trees, is one to two inches across and a deep orange-brown color.

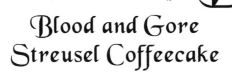

Blood and Gore Streusel Coffeecake

It oozes with "blood" and "innards" when you slice it!

1 cup (2 sticks)	butter or margarine, softened
1 cup	sugar
4 large	eggs
1-3/4 cups	flour
2 teaspoons	baking powder
2 teaspoons	grated lemon peel
1 1-1/2 pound can	raspberry pie filling
1 1-pound can	sliced cling peaches, drained

Preheat oven to 325 degrees Fahrenheit. Grease and flour a 9x13-inch cake pan.

In a large bowl beat butter and sugar at medium speed until smooth and lemon-colored. Beat in eggs, one at a time. Sift together flour and baking powder and gradually beat into egg mixture. Beat in lemon peel. Spread batter evenly in cake pan. Arrange peaches on top. Spread raspberry pie filling over peaches. Top with Streusel Topping. Bake 45 to 50 minutes until light golden in color. Cut into squares.

Streusel Topping

1/2 cup (1 stick)	butter or margarine
1 cup	flour
1/4 cup	sugar

Melt the butter. Stir in flour and sugar to form a soft dough. Pinch topping into tiny pieces and sprinkle over top of raspberry pie filling.

Time of Death

Crime novels often give the impression that time of death is easy to ascertain. In reality, this is not the case, although there are factors that can be used to give an estimate.

For example, a dead body will cool by approximately two and one-half degrees Fahrenheit per hour, reaching a uniform temperature with the environment after twenty-four hours. Lividity, staining caused by settling of the blood in the lower portions of the body, shows in three to five hours. Rigor mortis begins in one to four hours.

Be aware that, apart from rigor and lividity, stomach contents may be examined to determine how far digestion is advanced. So, make the final meal a memorable one!

Merfisa's Cosa Nostra Confection

More delicious than the perfect crime
and as easy to arrange as a mob hit.

1 large package	vanilla pudding (not instant)
	graham crackers
1 regular tub	Cool Whip

Prepare pudding according to directions on package. Line the bottom of a loaf pan or rectangular casserole dish with graham crackers. Spread a layer of hot pudding over crackers. Alternate layers of graham crackers and pudding, ending with pudding. Crumble graham crackers on top of final pudding layer. Refrigerate until *very* cold. Cut into thin slices, like a torte, and serve with whipped topping.

Variations: Use different flavor puddings, extracts such as vanilla or lemon, cinnamon graham crackers, or finely chopped nuts or shaved chocolate on top of pudding layers.

It is a sin to believe evil of others,
but it is seldom a mistake.

H.L. Mencken: *A Mencken Chrestomathy*

Don't Trifle with Me!

A traditional British poisoner's delight.

1-2 packages	jelly rolls
1 large can	fruit cocktail or sliced peaches
2-4 tablespoons	Harvey's Bristol Cream sherry
	Vanilla Custard
	whipped cream (optional)

Slice jelly rolls into 1-inch slices. Line the bottom of a deep dish with the slices. Sprinkle with sherry and let stand for 10 minutes. Drain the canned fruit and spoon over the jelly roll. Top with Vanilla Custard. Refrigerate. Garnish with whipped cream if desired.

Vanilla Custard

3/4 cup	sugar
2 tablespoons	cornstarch
1/8 teaspoon	salt
2 cups	half and half
4 large	egg yolks, well beaten
2 tablespoons	butter
1-1/2 teaspoons	vanilla
1 cup	heavy cream, whipped

Combine sugar, cornstarch, and salt in the top of a double boiler. Over medium heat, gradually stir in half and half. Cover and cook for 8 minutes without stirring. Uncover and cook another 10 minutes, stirring frequently. Stir in butter, egg yolks, and vanilla. Remove from heat and cool 5 minutes. Fold in whipped cream.

Thallium

Discovered in 1861 by Sir William Crookes, thallium is a heavy metal similar to lead. For the professional poisoner, thallium has several worthwhile properties: it dissolves in water, is almost tasteless, and its initial symptoms mimic the aches and pains of the flu.

Thallium has the convenience of being a cumulative poison, so it can be administered over a period of time. It does have one drawback—it causes loss of hair. If you feel tingling or numbness in extremities and noticeable hair loss, you would be advised to look twice at your nearest and dearest.

A Yummy Way to Die
Custard

A slim version of creme brulée, the perfect disguise
for a pinch of cyanide for the victim
who won't cheat on her diet.

2 cups	nonfat milk
2 tablespoons	nonfat powdered milk
3/4 cup	egg substitute
1/3 cup	sugar
1 teaspoon	vanilla
2 tablespoons	sugar

Preheat oven to 325 degrees Fahrenheit.

Blend together milk, powdered milk, egg substitute, sugar, and vanilla in a blender. Set custard mixture aside. Sprinkle the 2 tablespoons sugar in an 8-inch cake pan and heat over low heat until the sugar is melted and golden brown. Cool slightly. Pour custard in cake pan. Place in a pan filled with 1-inch of hot water. Bake 1 hour or until custard is set. Chill and unmold to serve.

Everybody is a potential murderer.
I've never killed anyone, but I frequently get satisfaction
reading the obituary notices.

Clarence Darrow in an interview

Chocolate Shriek Cookies

2 cups (4 sticks)	butter
2 cups	sugar
2 cups	brown sugar
4 large	eggs
2 teaspoons	vanilla
4 cups	flour
5 cups	ground oatmeal *
1 teaspoon	salt
2 teaspoons	baking powder
2 teaspoons	baking soda
24 ounces	chocolate chips
1 8-ounce	Hershey bar, grated
3 cups	chopped nuts

Preheat oven to 375 degrees Fahrenheit. Grease cookie sheets.

Cream butter and sugars. Add eggs and vanilla. Mix together with flour, oatmeal, salt, baking powder, and soda. Add chocolate chips, Hershey bar, and nuts. Roll into balls and place 2 inches apart on cookie sheets. Bake 10 minutes. Makes 112 cookies. Recipe may be halved.

*Ground oatmeal: process oatmeal to a fine powder in a blender.

I came to the conclusion
many years ago that almost all crime
is due to the repressed desire for aesthetic expression.

Evelyn Waugh: *Decline and Fall*

Assassination Apple Cake

Will disguise just about any deadly dose.

1/2 cup	flour, sifted
3/4 cup	brown sugar, firmly packed
1 teaspoon	baking powder
1/4 teaspoon	salt
dash	cinnamon
1 large	egg
1/2 teaspoon	vanilla
1 cup	apples, chopped
1/2 cup	walnuts, chopped

Preheat oven to 350 degrees Fahrenheit. Grease an 8-inch cake pan.

Mix together flour, brown sugar, baking powder, salt, and cinnamon. Stir in egg and vanilla and mix well. Fold in apples and walnuts. The batter will be stiff, almost like drop-cookie dough. Spread batter in cake pan and bake 25 to 30 minutes.

Wisteria

Wisteria floribunda is native to Japan, but common throughout the United States. A deciduous creeper that may attain forty-five feet in length, it has many drooping leaflets and violet or white flowers. All parts of this attractive plant are poisonous.

Chocolate Super Sin Pastry

Sin today for tomorrow you die...

1 sheet	puff pastry, frozen
8 ounces	semisweet chocolate chips
1/3 cup	walnuts, chopped
1 tablespoon	butter
	powdered sugar

Preheat oven to 425 degrees Fahrenheit.

Thaw pastry for 20 minutes, then roll out on a floured board to a 12- to 14-inch square. Place chocolate chips, walnuts, and butter in the center. Pull pastry edges together, twist, and put on an ungreased cookie sheet. Bake 20 minutes. Let stand 10 minutes, then sprinkle with powdered sugar.

Effective Lying

The ability to lie effectively is of inestimable value to anyone guilty of desserticide.

The verbal and non-verbal cues that indicate someone is lying include nervous mannerisms (licking lips), hesitating before answering questions, giving brief replies, avoiding eye contact, and shifting posture frequently.

Practice your lying. When interrogated, keep your hands still, even though tempted to fiddle with something. Do not stare fixedly at the investigator, but meet his or her glance in a natural manner. Do not make vague, sweeping statements, but reply to questions with factual statements. If you sense that a question may trap you, frown and say something like, "I'm sorry, I can't quite remember..."

In for the Kill Tiramisu

6 ounces	espresso coffee, made very strong
3 tablespoons	Marsala wine
48	ladyfingers
4 large	egg yolks or equivalent egg substitute
1-1/2 cups	superfine sugar (or use regular sugar, pulverized in the blender)
2 cups	Mascarpone cheese
1 cup	Ricotta cheese
1 cup	heavy whipping cream
3 tablespoons	unsweetened cocoa powder (Dutch process)

Mix the coffee with 1 tablespoon Marsala wine, then brush the mixture evenly over all the ladyfingers. Set aside. Beat egg yolks, slowly adding 1 cup sugar, until the mixture is smooth. Add the Mascarpone and Ricotta cheeses, blending well. Blend in 1/4 cup sugar and the remaining 2 tablespoons Marsala wine. Set aside. Whip cream until stiff. Fold in remaining 1/4 cup sugar, mixing well. Set aside.

Place 24 ladyfingers in the bottom of a rectangular glass dish. Spread with half of the egg yolk-cheese mixture, then half the whipping cream. Repeat the layers in the same order with the remaining mixtures. Dust the top with cocoa powder. Refrigerate *at least 6 hours* or overnight, before serving.

If once a man indulges himself in murder,
very soon he comes to think little of robbing;
and from robbing he next comes to drinking
and Sabbath-breaking,
and from that to incivility and procrastination.

Thomas de Quincey: *Murder Considered as One of the Fine Arts*

Hit Woman Gingerbread

You'll die happy.

2 cups	flour
2 teaspoons	baking powder
1/4 teaspoon	baking soda
1/4 teaspoon	salt
2 teaspoons	ground ginger
1 teaspoon	cinnamon
1/3 cup	shortening or margarine
1/2 cup	sugar
1 large	egg
3/4 cup	molasses
3/4 cup	sour milk

Preheat oven to 350 degrees Fahrenheit. Grease an 8x8x2-inch cake pan. Thoroughly combine the flour, baking powder, soda, salt, and spices. Set aside. Cream shortening and sugar together. Add egg and beat until fluffy. Stir in molasses. Alternately add dry ingredients and sour milk, stirring gently until just blended. Batter will be thick. Turn into cake pan and make sure it fills the corners. Bake 45 to 50 minutes or until the bread springs back when gently pressed in the center.

Serve hot, warm, or cold, though cutting it nicely when hot takes a bit of practice. Top with whipped cream, ice cream, your favorite fruit sauce, or dust with powdered sugar.

Rigor Mortis

The source of the term "stiff" for a dead person.

Brought about by the coagulation of protein in the muscles, it begins in the jaw and eyelids one to four hours after death and gradually spreads to the rest of the body. Full rigor is achieved after about twelve hours. It lasts for twelve hours, then gradually disappears over another twelve hours. Once rigor mortis is gone, it cannot return.

Be careful to arrange your victim in a tidy fashion, especially if you intend to dispose of the body.

It's Curtains!
Chocolate Cake
with Frantic Frosting

1 box	chocolate cake mix with pudding in the mix
	Frantic Frosting (recipe follows)
	Raspberry Sauce (recipe follows)
	chocolate curls

Prepare cake according to package directions. Bake in two round pans. Cool. Spread layers with Frantic Frosting and assemble. Allow to set. Spoon Raspberry Sauce over cake and onto the serving plate. Garnish with chocolate curls.

Frantic Frosting

8 tablespoons	cocoa
1-1/2 cups	sugar
1/2 teaspoon	salt
1/4 to 1/2 cup	milk
1 teaspoon	brandy
2 tablespoons	butter

In saucepan, blend together cocoa, sugar, salt, and 1/4 cup milk. Cook, stirring often, over low heat until almost thick. Add additional milk if too thick. Add butter and brandy, and beat until stiff.

(Continued)

Raspberry Sauce

1 bag	frozen raspberries
1/2 cup	sugar
2 teaspoons	water
	sugar

In a saucepan, cook raspberries, sugar, and water over low heat until raspberries break up, approximately 10 minutes. Remove from heat. Puree. Put back into the pan, reheat, adding additional sugar until sauce thickens. Cool.

An Ugly Way to Go Cake

1 box	yellow cake mix
1/2 cup (1 stick)	margarine, softened
2 large	eggs

Preheat oven to 350 degrees Fahrenheit. Grease and flour an 11x13-inch cake pan.

Beat together cake mix, margarine, and eggs. Batter will be stiff. Spread in cake pan. Spread Cream Cheese Topping over batter. Bake 35 minutes or until a toothpick inserted in the center comes out clean.

Cream Cheese Topping

8 ounces	cream cheese
1 pound	powdered sugar
1/2 cup (1 stick)	margarine, softened

Combine ingredients and mix well.

Malice Aforethought

Murder is defined as "the unlawful killing of a human being with malice aforethought." Malice aforethought is the deliberate intention to unlawfully take away the life of someone else.

Although the term gives the impression that you have *planned* the death of your victim, this is not the case. In contrast to accidental death, malice aforethought simply means that you had intent to do your victim harm that could result in death.

Be aware that the use of poison shows deliberate premeditation and so fulfills the requirements of malice aforethought. Find an explanation for how the poison accidentally appeared in your victim's dessert.

The Devil Made Me Do It
Chocolate Chip Cheesecake

Every forkful is to die for, each chocolate chip another coffin nail to seal your victim's fate.

1 cup	graham cracker crumbs
3 tablespoons	sugar
3 tablespoons	margarine or butter
3 8-ounce packages	cream cheese, softened
3/4 cup	sugar
3 large	eggs
1 cup	small semisweet chocolate chips
1 teaspoon	vanilla

Preheat oven to 450 degrees Fahrenheit.

Combine graham cracker crumbs, sugar, and margarine well. Press into the bottom of a 9-inch spring form pan. Combine cream cheese and sugar at medium speed until well blended. Add eggs one at a time. Mix well. Add chocolate chips and vanilla. Pour over crust. Bake 10 minutes at 450 degrees, then reduce heat to 250 degrees and bake 35 minutes longer. Loosen cake from rim of pan. Cool before removing from pan. Chill before serving.

Antimony (Tarter Emetic)

Known since ancient times, antimony was used in cosmetics in Egypt and by medieval monks to reduce appetite when fasting.

Colorless and almost tasteless, antimony was the poison of choice in several famous Victorian murder cases, as its effects conveniently mimicked gastroenteritis. Medicinally, it was used to induce vomiting, so care had to be taken by a poisoner not to overdose the victim, as antimony would be expelled before it could kill.

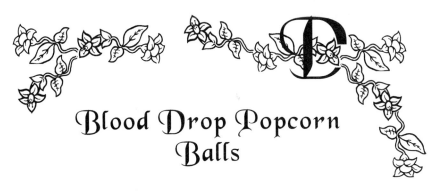

Blood Drop Popcorn Balls

Pass these out at Halloween or your next mystery party to provide a little sweet horror.

2 cups	sugar
1/2 teaspoon	salt
1 cup	light corn syrup
1 cup	water
1 teaspoon	vinegar
3 tablespoons	butter or margarine
5 quarts	popped corn
1 large bag	red licorice pieces
	oil, to grease fingers

Combine sugar, salt, corn syrup, water, vinegar, and butter. Cook over low heat to the hard ball state (250 degrees Fahrenheit on a candy thermometer). In a large oven-proof bowl, combine popped corn with licorice pieces. Pour hot syrup slowly over popcorn and licorice. Mix carefully to coat all pieces. Grease your fingers and shape mixture into balls. Cool and wrap in red cellophane if desired.

Positive Self-Presentation

If you are a suspect in a crime, it is important to present yourself in a positive light to any police officers you encounter.

Think of the situation as a job interview where you want to make the most favorable impression possible. You will be viewed as a package of spoken and nonspoken signals. Be sure that what you say and how you act fit seamlessly together.

Maintain a high level of eye contact, lean forward, and keep an appropriate facial expression. Smiling should be avoided. Indications of subdued shock or distress can be effective. Be careful not to overact as this may create suspicion, not lessen it.

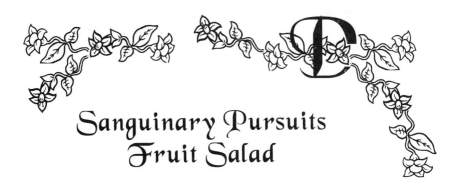

Sanguinary Pursuits
Fruit Salad

Boysenberries will be boysenberries.

1 package	raspberry gelatin
1 cup	boiling water
1 cup	unsweetened applesauce
1 cup	stewed or frozen boysenberries
	whipped cream (optional)

Dissolve the gelatin in boiling water. Cool until syrupy. Stir in remaining ingredients and chill until thick. If you can't find boysenberries, you can substitute frozen, unsweetened raspberries, although this will make the dessert less "boysenous." You may increase its lethality by serving it with whipped cream.

If this dish is served at a Midwest potluck, be sure to get your share early because any kind of gelatin dessert (particularly if it includes marshmallows) is considered salad, and this one is too good to miss.

Crimes, like virtues, are their own rewards.

George Farquhar: *The Inconstant*

Almond-Orange Tumult

Quick and easy for both the cook and the victim.

2 large	oranges
6 large	eggs
1-1/2 cups	ground almonds
1 cup	sugar
1 teaspoon	baking powder
	whipped cream (optional)

Preheat oven to 400 degrees Fahrenheit. Butter and flour an 8-inch cake pan.

Boil the oranges (unpeeled) in water for 2 hours. Process the oranges in food processor to make a pulp. Add the eggs, almonds, sugar, and baking powder. Process again to mix well. Turn batter into cake pan. Bake about 60 minutes or until a toothpick inserted in the center comes out clean.

This is a very moist, delicious cake with a strong orange flavor, just the thing to mask your lethal ingredient. A dollop of whipped cream on top makes it extra special if you don't care about calories—and your victim will be beyond worrying about his weight very soon!

Disposing of the Body: General Pointers

There are two principal reasons for disposing of the body:

Short-term—to conceal the crime long enough for you to either escape or concoct a suitable alibi.

Long-term—to ensure that your victim is never found and identified.

A cautionary note: Be aware that even if your victim's body is disposed of so effectively that it is never found, this does not guarantee your safety. It doesn't seem quite fair, but murder charges can be pursued and a conviction obtained, even if the body is missing.

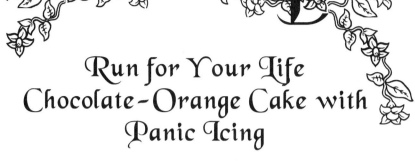

Run for Your Life
Chocolate-Orange Cake with
Panic Icing

2 cups	flour
2 cups	sugar
1 teaspoon	baking soda
1/2 cup	buttermilk or soured milk (add 1 teaspoon vinegar to the milk)
1 teaspoon	vanilla
1 teaspoon	orange extract
2 large	eggs
dash	salt
1 cup (2 sticks)	margarine
1 cup	water
1/4 cup	unsweetened cocoa
	Panic Icing (recipe follows)

Preheat oven to 400 degrees Fahrenheit. Grease and flour an 11x16-inch jelly roll pan.

Beat together flour, sugar, baking soda, buttermilk, vanilla, orange extract, eggs, and salt. Melt margarine in a 2-quart sauce pan. Add water and cocoa. Bring to boil. Stir into flour mixture. Beat together until smooth. Turn batter into the jelly roll pan. Bake 14 to 17 minutes or until top springs back when pressed. Frost with Panic Icing.

(Continued)

Panic Icing

1 pound	powdered sugar
1/2 cup (1 stick)	margarine, softened
1/2 cup	unsweetened cocoa
5 tablespoons	milk
1 teaspoon	vanilla
1 teaspoon	orange extract

Combine ingredients in a bowl. Beat until smooth.

Pharaoh's Curse Konafa

1 pound	konafa* pastry (found in Middle Eastern markets)
1 cup (2 sticks)	butter, melted and cooled
	Cream Filling (recipe follows)
	Syrup (recipe follows)

Preheat oven to 350 degrees Fahrenheit. Grease a 9x13-inch cake pan.

Place the konafa pastry in a large bowl. With your fingers, carefully pull out and separate the strands as much as possible so they no longer stick together too much. Pour melted butter over the loosened mass. Work it in thoroughly with your fingers, pulling and mixing so each strand is entirely coated with butter. Put half the pastry into the cake pan. Spread Cream Filling evenly over pastry. Cover the filling with the rest of the pastry, evening it out and flattening it with the palm of your hand. Bake 35 to 45 minutes at 350 degrees, then raise oven temperature to 450 degrees for 10 to 15 minutes longer until the pastry is a light golden color. Remove from the oven and pour half of the cold Syrup over the hot konafa. Wait 10 minutes; pour remaining Syrup over the konafa. Let stand 1 to 8 hours. Cut in 2-inch squares or diamond shapes to serve.

(Continued)

*Pronounced ko-NAH-fa. The raw dough looks like unbaked shredded wheat, but it is actually phyllo "spaghetti" rather than sheets.

Cream Filling

4 tablespoons	rice flour (or grind rice in blender until it's flour)
2 tablespoons	sugar
2-1/2 cups	milk
1/2 cup	heavy cream

Mix rice flour and sugar with 1/2 cup milk until it is a smooth paste. Boil the rest of the milk and add the rice paste slowly, stirring vigorously. Simmer while stirring, until mixture is very thick. Allow to cool, add the heavy cream, and mix well.

Syrup*

1-1/4 cups	sugar
1/2 cup	water
1 tablespoon	lemon juice
1 tablespoon	orange blossom water

Stir sugar, water, and lemon juice over moderate heat. Simmer until it thickens and coats the spoon. Stir in orange blossom water and cook for 2 minutes more. Cool completely.

*You might try 1-1/2 times the syrup. You want this dessert very moist, but not swimming in syrup.

Out of Control Yogurt Coffeecake

Run amok with yogurt.

1 box (18-1/2 ounces)	yellow cake mix (no pudding in mix)
1 cup	plain whole milk yogurt
1/2 cup	water
2 large	eggs
1 cup	walnuts or pecans, chopped
2 teaspoons	ground cinnamon
1/2 cup	sugar

Preheat oven according to cake mix package directions. Grease and flour a 9x13-inch cake pan.

Prepare cake mix according to package directions, substituting the yogurt for 1 cup water. Pour half the batter into the cake pan. Combine nuts, cinnamon, and sugar. Sprinkle half over the batter. Top with remaining batter and nut mixture. Bake according to package directions. Cool in the pan. This is a lighter version of sour cream coffee-cake—with 300 less calories!

Interrogation Techniques: The Bluff

This technique may be used to break your alibi and/or prove you are lying about one thing (and therefore may be lying about other, more important things).

For example, if you claim you were at a particular movie at the time the victim died, the investigator might say, "What did you do when the fire alarm sounded?" This is the bluff— there was no fire alarm. You will be watched closely to see if you delay in answering since someone who is lying will not be sure whether the incident occurred or not.

Serial Killer Cookies

1/2 cup	shortening
1 teaspoon	salt
1 teaspoon	vanilla
3/4 cup	sugar
2 large	eggs, well beaten
2-1/2 cups	flour, sifted

Preheat oven to 350 degrees Fahrenheit. Butter cookie sheets.

Combine shortening, salt, and vanilla. Add sugar and eggs, beating well. Add flour and mix well. Chill thoroughly. Roll out on a lightly floured board until 1/4-inch thick. Dip cookie cutter in flour before cutting each cookie. Place cookies on cookie sheets and bake about 8 minutes until delicately browned.

Beating Lie Detectors

Generally speaking, the results of a polygraph examination are not admissible in a court of law, but investigators may use them to ascertain what you may be lying about.

Your pulse rate and breathing patterns are monitored and appear as a series of graphs. The concept behind the lie detector is that tension created by telling a lie will be reflected in rises in blood pressure, breathing rate, and sweat production. Investigators will ask you a series of innocuous questions to establish a "base" response, then watch your responses to incriminating questions.

How to beat the system? On random questions, tighten your muscles (to raise blood pressure) and breathe more rapidly as you answer. With a little application you will ensure that your responses are too confusing to be of use!

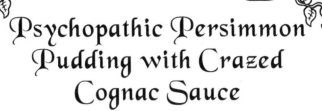

Psychopathic Persimmon Pudding with Crazed Cognac Sauce

1 cup	sugar
1/2 cup (1 stick)	butter, melted
1/4 teaspoon	salt
1 cup	flour, sifted
1/4 teaspoon	ground nutmeg
1/4 teaspoon	ground cinnamon
1 cup	pureed persimmon pulp (1 or 2 large, very ripe persimmons)
2 teaspoons	baking soda
2 teaspoons	warm water
3 tablespoons	cognac
1 teaspoon	vanilla
2 large	eggs, lightly beaten
1 cup	dried apricots
1/2 cup	pecans, chopped
	Crazed Cognac Sauce (recipe follows)

Butter a 5-to-6-cup oven-proof mold, making sure the inside surfaces are completely coated. Cut the dried apricots into sixths and set aside. Dissolve baking soda in warm water and set aside.

Melt butter in a 3-quart saucepan. Stir in sugar. Sift together flour, nutmeg, salt, and cinnamon and stir into butter mixture. Stir in persimmon pulp. Stir in baking soda mixture, cognac, vanilla, and eggs. Add apricots and pecans,

(Continued)

stirring until mixed. Pour into the mold. Cover and place in Dutch oven. Pour boiling water into Dutch oven to reach halfway up sides of mold. Cover Dutch oven and simmer 2-1/2 to 3 hours*. Remove the pudding mold from Dutch oven and let stand a few minutes before unmolding onto serving dish. Serve with Crazed Cognac Sauce.

Crazed Cognac Sauce

1 large	egg or equivalent egg substitute
1/2 cup (1 stick)	butter, melted
1 cup	powdered sugar, sifted
dash	salt
1 tablespoon	cognac (or brandy flavoring**)
1 cup	whipping cream

Beat egg until fluffy and light. Beat in butter, powdered sugar, salt, and cognac. Whip cream until stiff. Gently fold into egg mixture. Cover and chill. May be stored up to 2 weeks in refrigerator.

*Recipe may be halved; if cut in half, simmer 2 hours.

**Warning: Children love this sauce. You may want to substitute brandy flavoring because of this.

Reasonable Doubt Bread Pudding

4 cups	stale cinnamon rolls, coffee cake, or bread
3 cups	milk, warmed
pinch	salt
3 large	eggs, separated
1/2 cup	sugar
1 teaspoon	vanilla
1/2 teaspoon	nutmeg
1/2 cup	raisins
1/4 cup	orange or lemon marmalade (optional)

Preheat oven to 350 degrees Fahrenheit. Grease a large baking dish.

Dice the stale bread into cubes. Cover with the warm milk. Add salt. Beat together the sugar, egg yolks, vanilla, and nutmeg. Stir in raisins and marmalade. Stir this mixture into the soaked bread. Beat the egg whites until stiff. Fold into the bread mixture. Pour the pudding into the baking dish. Place this dish in a large pan. Add 1/2-inch hot water to the large pan. Bake 50 to 60 minutes until pudding is set.

What Antacid Way to Go

Researchers for the Food and Drug Administration warn that gulping down mouthfuls of indigestion remedies may be fatal.

Excessive use of antacids may lead to magnesium poisoning. Symptoms can include weakness, drowsiness, confusion, clumsiness, paralysis, and coma.

As a means of murder, magnesium poisoning would be difficult to prove. This is a suitable poison if you are a very bad cook: make your dessert even less digestible than usual, then encourage your victim to consume vast quantities of antacid.

I Didn't Do It! Peanut Butter Fudge Cake

2 cups	boiling water
4 1-ounce squares	unsweetened baking chocolate
2 cups	sugar
2/3 cup	butter or margarine, softened
2 large	eggs
2 teaspoons	vanilla
3 cups	flour
1 teaspoon	baking powder
1-1/2 teaspoons	baking soda
1 cup	semisweet chocolate chips
1 cup	peanut butter chips
	Chocolate Glaze (recipe follows)
	Peanut Butter Glaze (recipe follows)

Preheat oven to 350 degrees Fahrenheit. Grease a 12-cup Bundt pan.

Pour boiling water over unsweetened chocolate. Do not stir. Set aside; cool to lukewarm. Cream sugar and butter until smooth. Beat in eggs and vanilla. Drain water from chocolate, reserving liquid. Blend melted chocolate into creamed mixture. Combine flour, baking powder, and baking soda. Add to creamed mixture alternately with reserved liquid from chocolate. Beat thoroughly at low speed after each addition. Stir in chocolate and peanut butter chips. Turn into pan. Bake 50 to 55 minutes or until toothpick inserted in center comes out clean.

(Continued)

Cool 15 minutes; remove from pan. Cool completely before glazing. Spoon Chocolate Glaze over entire cake. Refrigerate until glaze is firm. Drizzle with Peanut Butter Glaze. Refrigerate.

Chocolate Glaze

1/4 cup (1/2 stick)	margarine or butter
2 tablespoons	water
3 tablespoons	light corn syrup
2 teaspoons	vanilla
1 cup	semisweet chocolate chips
1/4 cup	powdered sugar, sifted

In medium saucepan combine margarine, water, corn syrup, and vanilla. Heat to boiling. Add chocolate chips. Cover and remove from heat. Let stand 5 minutes. Remove lid. Stir mixture until smooth. Stir in powdered sugar until blended. Chill 10 minutes or until glaze is of spreading consistency.

Peanut Butter Glaze

3/4 cup	powdered sugar, sifted
2 tablespoons	peanut butter
2 to 3 tablespoons	hot whipping cream or milk

In small bowl blend powdered sugar, peanut butter, and cream.

Kill 'Em with Cookies

1 cup	shortening
1 cup	sugar
1 large	egg
1 cup	molasses
4 cups	flour
2 teaspoons	soda
1/2 teaspoon	salt
2 teaspoons	ginger
1/2 teaspoon	cinnamon
1/4 teaspoon	cloves

Preheat oven to 350 degrees Fahrenheit. Grease cookie sheets.

Thoroughly cream shortening and sugar. Add eggs and mix well. Stir in molasses. Sift together dry ingredients and combine with molasses mixture. Chill thoroughly. Roll into 1-inch diameter balls. Roll balls in sugar, then place 2 inches apart on cookie sheets. Bake 18 to 20 minutes. Remove from cookie sheets and cool on racks.

Singularity is almost invariably a clue.
The more featureless and commonplace a crime is,
the more difficult it is to bring it home.

Arthur Conan Doyle: *The Adventures of Sherlock Holmes*

An Arresting Chocolate Cake

So easy, you can make it with one arm handcuffed to a post!

1/2 cup (1 stick)	butter
1 cup	sugar
4 large	eggs
16-ounce can	Hershey brand chocolate syrup
1 cup	flour, sifted
1 teaspoon	baking powder
1 teaspoon	vanilla
	powdered sugar (optional)

Preheat oven to 350 degrees Fahrenheit. Grease and flour a tube pan.

Cream butter and sugar. Beat in eggs one at a time. Stir in chocolate syrup (it's the liquid). Fold in flour and baking powder. Beat at low speed. Stir in vanilla. Bake 40 to 50 minutes or until a toothpick inserted in center comes out clean. Cool 10 minutes. Turn out on rack and cool.

To gild the lily, sprinkle with confectioner's sugar before it is completely cool.

Ricin

A plant toxin derived from castor beans, ricin was seriously considered (but never used) as a chemical weapon during World War II. Ricin causes toxemia, similar to that caused by bacteria. Even in minute doses it is fatal and is almost undetectable in the body.

The most notorious use of ricin occurred in the late seventies in the famous Bulgarian Umbrella case. Georgi Markov, a Bulgarian defector, was stabbed in the leg with an umbrella while waiting for a bus in London. A tiny pellet of ricin deposited in the puncture wound slowly released the poison into Markov's bloodstream. He died four days later.

Pernicious Peanut Butter Cookies

1/4 cup	shortening
1/4 cup (1/2 stick)	butter
1 cup	chunky peanut butter
1/2 cup	granulated sugar
1/2 cup	brown sugar
1 large	egg
1 1/4 cup	flour
3/4 teaspoon	baking soda
1/2 teaspoon	baking powder
1/4 teaspoon	salt

Preheat oven to 375 degrees Fahrenheit. Lightly grease cookie sheets.

Mix thoroughly butter, shortening, peanut butter, granulated sugar, brown sugar, and egg. Blend in flour, soda, baking powder, and salt. Cover and chill. Shape chilled dough into 1-inch balls. Place balls 3 inches apart on cookie sheet. Using a fork dipped in flour, flatten balls to 2-inch rounds, making a crisscross pattern with the tines. Bake 10 to 12 minutes or until set but not hard. Cool on racks.

Death Row Modification: Substitute 1/4 cup butter for the shortening.

If You Are Unlucky Enough to Be Arrested...

You have the right to remain silent. You do not have to answer any questions, but you may decide that a cooperative stance will be to your advantage.

Any statement you make (spoken or written) can be used against you.

You have the right to speak with an attorney and to have an attorney present when you are questioned.

If you want, but can't afford, an attorney, one must be provided without charge before any interrogation can begin.

IMPORTANT: Take careful note of whether you have been advised of your Miranda rights when taken into custody. If you have not had your rights read to you, do NOT point this out. Anything you say or do will not be admissible in a court of law!

Sneak Attack Carrot Cake

With five (count 'em!) deadly spices.

1-1/2 cups	sugar
1 tablespoon	molasses
4 large	eggs
2 cups	flour
1 teaspoon	baking powder
1 teaspoon	baking soda
1/2 teaspoon	salt
2 teaspoons	cinnamon
1/2 teaspoon	ginger
1/2 teaspoon	cloves
1/4 teaspoon	nutmeg
1/4 teaspoon	cardamom
3/4 cup	oil
3 cups	grated carrots
1/2 cup	raisins
2/3 cup	walnuts, chopped
	Watch Your Back Frosting (recipe follows)

Preheat oven to 350 degrees Fahrenheit. Oil and flour one angel food cake pan, or one 9x13-inch cake pan, or two 8-inch layer pans.

Mix sugar, molasses, and eggs together with wire whisk. Sift the dry ingredients and stir into sugar mixture. Add 1/2 cup oil and the carrots and mix well. Add raisins, walnuts, and remaining oil, mixing well again. Pour batter into cake

(Continued)

pan(s). Bake 60 to 75 minutes for the large pans or 40 to 55 minutes for small pans. Cool 10 minutes. Turn out on rack and cool. Dust with powdered sugar or frost with Watch Your Back Frosting.

Watch Your Back Frosting

4 ounces	cream cheese
2 tablespoons	butter
1-1/2 cups	powdered sugar
1 tablespoon	cream
1 teaspoon	vanilla, brandy, or rum

Combine cream cheese, butter, powdered sugar, cream, and flavoring. Beat until smooth.

Violent Rummed Bananas

Follow your taste buds as to amounts.

2 to 4

ripe bananas
Meyer's Dark Rum
brown sugar
butter or margarine

Melt some butter in a sauté pan over medium-high heat. Slice bananas into the pan and let them cook until mushy. Add brown sugar—a couple of tablespoons, more if you have a sweet tooth. Stir, coating the bananas. Add a splash of rum—more if you like, but don't flood the pan. When dessert is bubbling, use a long fireplace match to flame the rum. Dessert is ready when nice and mushy.

This dessert is great by itself, but really terrific over ice cream (especially vanilla or coffee) or sponge cake.

There is no person who is not dangerous for someone.

Marie de Sevigne in a letter

You're a Dead Mousse

2/3 cup (4 ounces)	semisweet chocolate bits
2 tablespoons	strong coffee
2 tablespoons	Amaretto
1 teaspoon	vanilla
4 large	eggs, separated or equivalent egg substitute
1 tablespoon	sugar
2 tablespoons	slivered almonds or chocolate sprinkles
	chocolate leaves (optional)

Microwave chocolate and coffee in large bowl until chocolate melts when you stir it. Stir in Amaretto. Stir in egg yolks, one at a time. In another bowl, beat egg whites until soft peaks form. Add sugar and beat until stiff. Stir 1/3 of the egg whites into chocolate mixture, then fold in the rest carefully. Spoon mousse into 6 parfait or wine glasses. Cover with plastic wrap and chill at least 2 hours. Garnish with slivered almonds or chocolate sprinkles at serving time.

Bonus: Tastes like heaven and only 160 calories per serving! If you're in the mood, garnish with chocolate leaves.

To make chocolate leaves:

Spread melted (microwaved) semisweet chocolate bits on the underside of rinsed hibiscus or other nicely shaped leaves. Refrigerate until set, then gently peel off chocolate.

The Alibi

The word alibi is Latin for "elsewhere" and is a favored defense in both fiction and real life. An alibi is used to establish that you could not possibly have committed the crime because you were somewhere else at the time.

Take care if you ask someone to lie to establish your alibi—it's amazing how the threat of prosecution can encourage even your nearest and dearest to tell the inconvenient truth.

Another common problem is blackmail. The person providing your alibi correctly assumes that you have a keen interest in maintaining the deception and demands payment to keep quiet. In a worst-case scenario, you would be forced to commit yet another murder and go to the trouble of establishing a new alibi.

Fatally Fudgy Brownies

1 cup (2 sticks)	butter or margarine
4 1-ounce squares	unsweetened chocolate
2 cups	sugar
4 large	eggs
1 cup	flour
1 teaspoon	vanilla extract
1/2 teaspoon	salt (optional)
2 cups	nuts, coarsely chopped (optional)

Preheat over to 350 degrees Fahrenheit. Grease 9x13-inch cake pan.

In 3-quart saucepan over very low heat, melt butter and chocolate, stirring the mixture constantly. Remove pan from heat and stir the sugar into the chocolate with a spoon. Allow the mixture to cool slightly. Add eggs, one at a time, blending well after each addition. Stir in flour, vanilla, and salt. Add the chopped nuts and stir to blend well. Pour batter into cake pan, scraping the sides of saucepan with a rubber spatula. Bake 30 to 35 minutes or until a toothpick inserted in center comes out clean. Cool in pan on wire rack. Cut brownies into 24 squares with a sharp knife.

Alcohol

An extremely slow way to kill someone, but much fun can be had by all. Note that alcohol leads to a reduction in coordination, vision, memory, reasoning abilities, and judgment.

You might consider using alcohol in conjunction with a more rapid method of dispatch.

What a Way to Die Sour Cream Chocolate Cake

Chocolate lovers will dream about this one!

3 cups	cake flour
3 cups	sugar
3/4 cup	cocoa
3/4 cup (1-1/2 sticks)	butter, softened
3/4 cup	sour cream
1-1/2 cups	hot water
2-1/4 teaspoons	baking soda
3 large	eggs
2 teaspoons	vanilla
	ready-made sour cream chocolate frosting

Preheat oven to 350 degrees Fahrenheit. Line one 11x16-inch cake pan or two oversized round cake pans with waxed paper. (This batter won't fit in regular-size pans—the cake turns out very high and moist.)

Dissolve baking soda in the hot water and set aside. Sift the flour and set aside. Sift sugar into mixer bowl. Add cocoa, butter, and sour cream. Blend at medium speed; make sure beaters are in sour cream so cocoa won't fly. Add the eggs one at a time to sour cream mixture, beating well after each addition. Add vanilla. Reduce speed to low. Alternately beat in flour and baking soda-water mixture. Batter will be runny. Pour batter into cake pan. Bake 45 to 50 minutes until toothpick inserted in center comes out clean. Cool. Frost with ready-made sour cream chocolate frosting.

Arrival of the Law
at the Scene of the Crime

FBI statistics show that the faster law enforcement officers respond to a crime and begin preliminary investigations, the better the "solve" rate.

A thoughtful murderer will ensure that investigations are delayed as much as possible. This can be achieved by a) concealing the body or b) ensuring that your victim is discovered after considerable time has passed.

When reporting the death yourself, it can be advantageous to give the wrong address (you always have the excuse that you were confused and upset) to delay arrival of the authorities.

Manslaughter Mint Brownies

4 1-ounce squares	chocolate (bitter, semisweet, or unsweetened)
3/4 cup (1-1/2 sticks)	butter
1 heaping teaspoon	instant coffee
4 large	eggs
2 cups	sugar
1 tablespoon	vanilla
1 cup	flour
2 cups	mint chocolate chips
1 cup	walnuts or pecans, chopped
	powdered sugar (optional)

Preheat oven to 425 degrees Fahrenheit. Grease a 9x13-inch cake pan.

Melt chocolate, butter, and instant coffee using a microwave oven or double boiler. Stir and allow to cool to room temperature. In a small mixer bowl, beat eggs and sugar until creamy. In a large mixer bowl, combine cooled chocolate mixture and egg-sugar mixture. Beat well. Add vanilla. Add flour, about 1/4 cup at a time, beating after each addition. Stir in mint chocolate chips and nuts. Turn batter into the cake pan. Bake about 20 minutes until top has a crust and brownies pull away from the sides of the pan. Sprinkle with powdered sugar if desired. These brownies always seem better the second day—if they last that long!

Variations: Substitute butterscotch chips, toffee chips, or chocolate raspberry chips (made by Hershey and often hard to find but well worth the effort) for the mint chocolate chips.

Evidence

There are two classes of evidence: direct and circumstantial. An eyewitness provides direct evidence. Circumstantial evidence relates to facts from which it may be inferred that a crime has been committed.

Hearsay evidence, something one has heard secondhand, is usually inadmissible, except for confessions or dying declarations. Witnesses must stick to the facts as they know them and avoid personal opinions or assumptions. The only exception to this is in the case of expert witnesses who are permitted to give their informed opinions.

If you do your job right, only sheer bad luck would lead to direct evidence against you. In the case of circumstantial evidence, familiarization with forensic science and careful planning should suffice.

Amaretto Swoon Cheesecake

1 cup	graham cracker crumbs
1/2 cup	almonds, toasted and ground
1/4 cup (1/2 stick)	butter or margarine, melted
1/3 cup + 2 tablespoons	sugar, divided
1/3 cup + 4 tablespoons	Amaretto, divided
4 ounces	almond paste
2 tablespoons	flour
3 8-ounce packages	cream cheese
4 large	eggs, or equivalent egg substitute
1 cup	sour cream, regular or imitation
	sliced almonds (optional)

Preheat oven to 350 degrees Fahrenheit. Grease a 9-inch springform pan.

Allow cream cheese to soften at room temperature. Combine graham cracker crumbs, ground almonds, butter, 1 tablespoon sugar, and 1 tablespoon Amaretto. Press crust mixture onto bottom and up the sides of pan. Refrigerate crust. Combine almond paste, 1/3 cup sugar, and flour. Beat until smooth. Add 1/3 cup Amaretto and beat. Add softened cream cheese, one package at a time, and beat in. Add 1 egg at a time and beat in. Beat well until smooth. Pour batter into chilled crust. Bake 45 to 50 minutes. Cheesecake will not be fully set in center.

While cheesecake bakes, blend together sour cream, 3 tablespoons Amaretto, and 1 tablespoon sugar. Spread mixture over top of baked cake. Return to oven for 20 minutes or until center is firm. Cool at room temperature on rack for 1 hour, then refrigerate in pan for 4 hours. To serve, remove sides of pan and garnish with sliced almonds.

A jury consists of twelve persons
chosen to decide
who has the better lawyer.

Attributed to Robert Frost

Annihilation Apple Cake

4 cups (5 to 6)	Red Delicious apples, unpeeled, thinly sliced
1 cup	walnuts, chopped
2 cups	sugar
3/4 cup	oil
2 large	eggs
1 teaspoon	vanilla
2 cups	flour
1 teaspoon	baking soda
1/4 teaspoon	salt
2 teaspoons	cinnamon

Preheat oven to 350 degrees Fahrenheit. Grease a 9x13-inch cake pan.

Cream together sugar, oil, eggs, and vanilla. Sift in flour, baking soda, salt, and cinnamon. Mix well. Stir in apples and walnuts. Turn into cake pan. Bake 45 minutes until toothpick inserted in center comes out clean. Cool.

Feigning Insanity to Avoid a Murder Rap

It is wise to research the particular form of madness you will be using. Symptoms you might consider developing include:

Delirium—showing disorganized thinking, you ramble, make incoherent comments, and generally indicate that you have great difficulty in maintaining attention on what is going on around you.

Dementia—your ability to think is seriously impaired, particularly your judgment and abstract thought processes.

Behavior that indicates you are suffering from delusions and hallucinations is always useful.

Special Note: Unsporting prosecutors will try to trap you into showing sanity. Be consistent. Know your madness and stick to it!

Maniacal Mousse

1 envelope	unflavored gelatin
1 tablespoon	sugar
1/2 cup	milk
1 6-ounce package	semisweet chocolate chips
1 teaspoon	vanilla extract
1-1/2 cups	Cool Whip or other sweetened whipped topping

In medium saucepan, mix unflavored gelatin with sugar. Blend in milk. Let stand 1 minute. Stir over low heat until gelatin is completely dissolved, about 5 minutes. Add chocolate and continue cooking, stirring constantly, until chocolate is melted. With wire whisk beat mixture until chocolate is blended. Stir in vanilla. Pour into large bowl and chill, stirring occasionally until mixture mounds slightly when dropped from spoon. Fold in whipped topping. Turn into 6 dessert dishes; chill until set. Garnish with additional topping.

Manslaughter

Manslaughter is distinguished from murder as being the unlawful (but unintentional) killing of a human being *without* malice.

Voluntary manslaughter occurs when the killing results from "a sudden quarrel or the heat of passion."

Involuntary manslaughter has two divisions. First, killing "in the commission of an unlawful act, not amounting to a felony." Second—suitable for those using *Desserticide*—killing of someone because of the lack of due caution.

If you feign confusion over the dessert ingredients, you may be charged with involuntary manslaughter rather than murder.

Terror-Misu

3/4 cup	powdered sugar
2 cups	whipping cream
8 ounces	Mascarpone cheese
1 8- to 10-inch	angel food cake
1/4 cup	strong black coffee (espresso-like)
1/4 cup + 5 tablespoons	Kahlua or coffee-flavored liqueur, divided
	cocoa powder or grated chocolate

Whip the cream with 1/4 cup powdered sugar and 2 tablespoons Kahlua, until stiff peaks form. Set aside. Whip Mascarpone cheese with 1/2 cup powdered sugar and 3 tablespoons Kahlua until smooth. Fold 1/2 cup whipped cream mixture into the Mascarpone cheese mixture.

With a serrated knife, cut angel food cake into three layers. Prick lots of holes into all three layers. In a small bowl, combine coffee with 1/4 cup Kahlua. Place the bottom layer of the cake on a plate or in a soufflé dish. Drizzle coffee-Kahlua mixture over the layer. Spread with half of Mascarpone mixture. Place second layer on top of first. Drizzle with coffee-Kahlua mixture and spread with remaining Mascarpone mixture. Top with cake layer. Frost top with remaining whipped cream mixture and dust lightly with cocoa or grated chocolate. Chill for up to 2 hours before serving. May be made the day before and served chilled. Keep refrigerated.

Oh, what a tangled web we weave,
When first we practice to deceive!

Sir Walter Scott: *Marmion*

Shaky Alibi Apple Crumble

4 cups	Granny Smith apples, peeled and sliced
1/2 cup	brown sugar
1/2 cup	flour
2 tablespoons	lemon juice
1/2 cup (1 stick)	butter or margarine
1 teaspoon	cinnamon

Preheat oven to 350 degrees Fahrenheit. Lightly butter a glass baking dish.

Spread apple slices evenly over bottom of baking dish. Sprinkle lemon juice over apple slices. Cream together butter and brown sugar. Stir in flour and cinnamon until mixture is crumbly. Spread over the apples. Bake 30 minutes. Serve warm or cold.

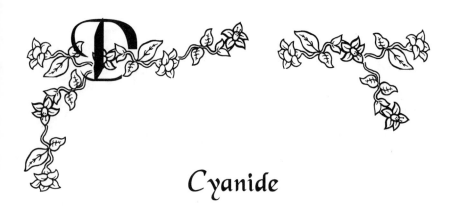

Cyanide

Potassium cyanide (prussic acid) acts very rapidly and so is popular as a means of suicide. It occurs as a plot device in many spy novels—rather than confess under torture, the spy bites on the capsule hooked over his or her molars. It was also the chosen method of suicide for Nazi war criminals Göring and Himmler.

Occurring naturally in stone fruits (within the kernel), such as the cherry and peach, it has a characteristic odor of bitter almonds. With a fatal dose, death occurs within four to five minutes as the respiratory center in the brain shuts down. In the form of prussic acid, it can kill within seconds.

Poisoners should delay official examination of victims, as cyanide changes chemically in the body and may be difficult to detect after time.

It'll Make You into an Angel Pie

4 large	egg whites
1/4 teaspoon	salt
1/4 teaspoon	cream of tartar
1 cup	granulated sugar
1/2 teaspoon	vanilla
1 small can	crushed pineapple, drained
1/2 cup	whipped cream

Preheat oven to 275 degrees Fahrenheit. Line a 9-inch pie pan or cookie sheet with brown paper.

Beat egg whites, salt, and cream of tartar until stiff. Add vanilla and beat in sugar, 1 spoonful at a time. Heap meringue mixture in the middle of pan and shape into a large pie shell with the high edges. Bake about 1 hour until the meringue is dry but not brown. Turn off the oven, open the door, and let meringue cool in the oven. Carefully remove the brown paper and put the meringue shell on a plate. Combine pineapple and whipped cream and spread on the meringue shell.

The pie may be kept in the refrigerator several hours or overnight; it only gets better!

Oleander

Found throughout the world, oleander (*Nerium oleander*) is often used in city landscaping because of its durability and appearance. An evergreen shrub growing six- to fourteen-feet tall, it has tough, narrow leaves and clusters of white, yellow, pink, salmon, or red flowers. All parts are poisonous, including the sap.

Malice Aforethought
Baked Apples

6 large	Golden Delicious apples
1/4 cup	brown sugar
1 tablespoon	cinnamon
1/4 cup	walnuts, chopped
1/4 cup	raisins
	butter

Preheat oven to 375 degrees Fahrenheit.

Wash and partially core the apples, leaving 1/2-inch at the base. Place the apples in a baking pan. Combine brown sugar, cinnamon, walnuts, and raisins. Fill the apples with this mixture. Dot with butter.

Pour 1/2-inch water into the bottom of the pan. Bake 45 minutes. Cool. Baste apples with the pan juices before serving.

Dying Declarations from Not-Quite-Dead Victims

If you are unfortunate enough to have a victim refuse to die, do try to discourage his or her declaration to a third party, particularly a police officer. Although such a declaration is hearsay evidence, it will be given special weight by the authorities and may be used at your trial.

Conditions for a dying declaration: 1. The victim must believe that he or she is definitely about to depart this life. (You should vigorously assure your victim that this is not the case!) 2. The victim must explain how he or she came to his/her present condition. (Announce that the victim is confused or mistaken.) 3. The victim must die. (A sigh of relief from you!)

Death Warrant Chocolate-Cherry Trifle

2 thin 8-inch layers	Foul Play Cocoa Fudge Cake (recipe follows)
	Choke-a-lot Pudding (recipe follows) or 1 large package pudding mix, made and set
	Coroner's Surprise Cherry Filling (recipe follows) or 2 16-ounce cans cherry pie filling
1 cup	heavy whipping cream
3 tablespoons	powdered sugar
1/2 teaspoon	vanilla

In the bottom of a 4-quart straight-sided, clear glass bowl, place one cake layer. Spoon half the Choke-a-lot Pudding over the cake. Spread half the Coroner's Surprise Cherry Filling over pudding. Layer the remaining cake, pudding, and cherry filling, as before. Whip the cream with the powdered sugar and vanilla. Spread over top layer of trifle. Chill before serving. Store covered in the refrigerator.

(Continued)

Foul Play Cocoa Fudge Cake

1/2 + 1/3 cup	flour
3/4 cup	granulated sugar
1/3 cup	cocoa powder
1/4 teaspoon	baking soda
1/2 teaspoon	salt
3/4 cup	buttermilk
1/4 cup	shortening
1/2 teaspoon	vanilla
1 large	egg

Preheat oven to 350 degrees Fahrenheit. Grease and flour two 8-inch round cake pans.

Combine ingredients in a mixing bowl. Beat at low speed for 30 seconds. Beat at high speed for 3 minutes. Divide into the cake pans. Bake 20 to 25 minutes until toothpick inserted in center comes out clean. Cool 10 minutes. Carefully turn out on racks and cool. Makes two thin layers.

Choke-a-lot Pudding

1/2 cup	cornstarch
2/3 cup	sugar
3 heaping tablespoons	cocoa powder
3 cups	milk

Combine cornstarch, sugar, and cocoa in a 3-quart sauce-pan. Gradually add milk and stir with whisk to remove lumps. Bring to a boil over medium heat, stirring constantly. Cook until thick, shiny and bubbly, about 5 minutes. Remove from heat and stir in vanilla. Allow to cool a few minutes and put waxed paper or plastic wrap on surface of pudding to prevent skin from forming. Cool.

(Continued)

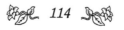

Coroner's Surprise Cherry Filling

2 1-pound cans	sour pie cherries, drained—reserve liquid
1-1/2 cups	cherry liquid (add water if necessary)
1/2 cup	cornstarch
1-1/2 cups	sugar
1/4 teaspoon	red food color (optional)

Combine sugar and cornstarch in a 3-quart saucepan. Gradually stir in cherry liquid and whisk to remove lumps. Bring to boil over medium heat, stirring frequently until mixture thickens and bubbles. Cook 2 minutes more. Add cherries and food coloring. Stir well and remove from heat. Mixture will be very thick. Cool.

The Perfect Murder

The perfect murder is not one where no one is ever tried and found guilty of the crime—that could be described as a wholly successful murder.

The truly *perfect* murder is the one that is never seen as murder in the first place. We can never know this, but perhaps a multitude of unknown murderers walk among us, smiling mildly as they contemplate their lethal achievements.

Life Behind Nanaimo Bars

A Canadian classic.

1/4 cup	granulated sugar
2 tablespoons	cocoa powder
1/2 cup (1 stick)	unsalted butter
1 large	egg
1 cup	graham cracker crumbs
1 cup	shredded coconut
1/2 cup	pecans, chopped
	Filling (recipe follows)
	Topping (recipe follows)

Line the bottom of an 8-inch square cake pan with parchment. In a large bowl, combine the sugar and cocoa. Melt the butter and pour it into the bowl; whisk to combine. Whisk in egg. Add the graham cracker crumbs, coconut, and pecan pieces. Mix well. (Don't worry if mixture seems a bit greasy.) Put this mixture into the prepared cake pan. Smooth with the back of a spoon to uniform thickness. Refrigerate.

Filling

3 tablespoons	unsalted butter
2-1/2 cups	powdered sugar, sifted
5 tablespoons	instant vanilla pudding mix
1/4 cup	milk

Cream butter with an electric mixer. Reduce speed to low and add powdered sugar about 1 tablespoon at a time. Scrape

(Continued)

down sides with spatula. Add pudding mix. Beat well. Add milk and beat until no lumps remain. Spread the filling over the base and return to refrigerator.

Topping

| 6 ounces | semisweet chocolate pieces |
| 2 teaspoons | unsalted butter |

Combine chocolate pieces and butter in a bowl and set over hot water or double boiler. Stir occasionally, making sure chocolate is smooth. Pour melted chocolate over filling and spread with spatula. Score surface into sixteen pieces and return to refrigerator.

When chilled, cut along the lines and ease bars out. Even then, you'll never get away.

This recipe was adapted from the *David Wood Good Food Book* by David Wood.

Index

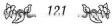

Delectable Desserts and Tongue-in-Cheek Advice for the Would-be Murderer

To order additional copies of *Desserticide*
use this form (or a facsimile):

Name _____

Address _____

City _____ State _____ Zip _____

Phone _____ Fax _____

Number of copies at $10 each _____

Total enclosed _____

Make your check out to SinC/LA and mail to:
Desserticide
P.O. Box 251646
Los Angeles, CA 90025
(213) 694-2972

Thanks For Your Order!